W9-AYB-553

A WORLD CONTENDER
Americans on the Global Stage 1900-1912

TITLE LIST

A WORLD CONTENDER

Americans on the Global Stage 1900-1912

BY
ERIC SCHWARTZ

MASON CREST PUBLISHERS
PHILADELPHIA

Mason Crest Publishers Inc.
370 Reed Road
Broomall, Pennsylvania 19008
(866) MCP-BOOK (toll free)

First printing
1 2 3 4 5 6 7 8 9 10

Schwartz, Eric.
  A world contender : Americans on the global stage (1900–1912) / by Eric Schwartz.
     p. cm. — (How America became America)
  Includes bibliographical references and index.
  Audience: Grades 9–12.
  ISBN 1-59084-911-6 ISBN 1-59084-900-0 (series)
  1. United States—Foreign relations—1901–1909—Juvenile literature. 2. Roosevelt, Theodore,
1858–1919—Juvenile literature. 3. United States—Foreign relations—1909–1913—Juvenile litera-
ture. 4. Wilson, Woodrow, 1856–1924—Juvenile literature. I. Title. II. Series.
  E756.S39 2004
  973.91'1'092—dc22
                         2004017056

Interior design by Dianne Hodack.
Produced by Harding House Publishing Service, Inc.
Cover design by Dianne Hodack.
Printed in the Hashemite Kingdom of Jordan.

CONTENTS

INTRODUCTION

by Dr. Jack Rakove

Today's America is not the same geographical shape as the first American colonies—and the concept of America has evolved as well over the years.

When the thirteen original states declared their independence from Great Britain, most Americans still lived within one or two hours modern driving time from the Atlantic coast. In other words, the Continental Congress that approved the Declaration of Independence on July 4, 1776, was continental in name only. Yet American leaders like George Washington, Benjamin Franklin, and Thomas Jefferson also believed that the new nation did have a continental destiny. They expected it to stretch at least as far west as the Mississippi River, and they imagined that it could extend even further. The framers of the Federal Constitution of 1787 provided that western territories would join the Union on equal terms with the original states. In 1803, President Jefferson brought that continental vision closer to reality by purchasing the vast Louisiana Territory from France. In the 1840s, negotiations with Britain and a war with Mexico brought the United States to the Pacific Ocean.

This expansion created great opportunities, but it also brought serious costs. As Americans surged westward, they created a new economy of family farms and large plantations. But between the Ohio River and the Gulf of Mexico, expansion also brought the continued growth of plantation slavery for millions of African Americans. Political struggle over the extension of slavery west of the Mississippi was one of the major causes of the Civil War that killed hundreds of thousands of Americans in the 1860s but ended with the destruction of slavery. Creating opportunities for American farmers also meant displacing Native Americans from the lands their ancestors had occupied for centuries. The opening of the west encouraged massive immigration not only from Europe but also from Asia, as Chinese workers came to labor in the California Gold Rush and the building of the railroads.

By the end of the nineteenth century, Americans knew that their great age of territorial expansion was over. But immigration and the growth of modern industrial cities continued to change the American landscape. Now Americans moved back and forth across the continent in search of economic opportunities. African Americans left the South in massive numbers and settled in dense concentrations in the cities of the North. The United States remained a magnet for immigration, but new immigrants came increasingly from Mexico, Central America, and Asia.

Ever since the seventeenth century, expansion and migration across this vast landscape have shaped American history. These books are designed to explain how this process has worked. They tell the story of how modern America became the nation it is today.

Theodore Roosevelt (left)
Great White Fleet Ship (right)

One
THE ROOSEVELT PRESIDENCY

On February 22, 1901, sixteen gleaming white ships sailed in a parade seven miles long. President Theodore Roosevelt watched proudly from the deck of the presidential yacht as the ships returned home after their fourteen-month voyage around the world. The ships, manned by more than 14,000 sailors, had covered some 43,000 miles and had made twenty port calls on six continents. The "Great White Fleet" (as the ships came to be known) was Teddy Roosevelt's announcement to the world: The United States is a power with which to be reckoned!

The voyage of the fleet was an *emblem* of the country's presence on the world stage, right where Teddy Roosevelt wanted America to be. The seeds of the nation's growth had been planted earlier, but Roosevelt had pushed the United States into a new active role in world affairs. During the early twentieth century, expansionism was the word many Americans used to define what they wanted for their country.

*An **emblem** is a symbol.*

Imperialism is the policy of seeking to dominate the affairs of weaker countries.

Ideals are standards of excellence.

Theodore Roosevelt

Teddy Roosevelt's "big stick"

10

After all, Americans wanted their country to be great—and in their minds, the way for American to be great was for it to grow . . . bigger and bigger and bigger. By the end of the nineteenth century, the United States had already spread from the East Coast to the West Coast. So where else could it spread?

Americans like Teddy Roosevelt began looking at lands across the ocean. If the United States expanded still larger, it would gain glory and power. And it would bring its ideas about democracy and freedom to other people. In other words, reasoned Roosevelt and other Americans, if the United States exerted its control over other nations, it would really be doing them a favor.

Imperialism is another word for this attitude. The British government had gone in for imperialism in a big way; their government's power and influence had extended around the globe. Other nations were building smaller empires, and the United States did not want to be left out. Americans wanted to prove to the rest of the world that the United States was no longer a young nation too immature to have power. They felt they were ready to take their place with the "grown-ups."

Not all Americans agreed with this way of

A postcard commemorates one of the Great White Fleet

thinking. These people were called anti-imperialists, and they were convinced that America should mind its own business and not stick its nose into other nations' affairs. They remembered that Thomas Jefferson, one of the founding fathers, had said: "If there is one principle more deeply rooted in the mind of every American, it is that we should have nothing to do with conquest." They felt that American *ideals* called for the United States to be different from the other countries. According to one anti-imperialist, Carl Schulz, a former senator, America should be "the example and guiding star" of humanity by pursuing peace and harmony between nations.

Teddy Roosevelt in the Rough Riders during the Spanish-American War

12

Imperialists like Teddy Roosevelt countered with arguments like this:

Those who do not want the United States to annex foreign lands tell us we ought not to govern a people without their consent. I answer, "That rule of government applies only to those people who are capable of self-government."

These are ideas that are still being hashed out today in twenty-first-century America. Does the United States have a responsibility to help other nations run their affairs according to our own beliefs? Should America act as a kind of global police officer, making sure the nations of the world behave themselves? Is it right for America's power to grow and grow—or should a nation's power have limits? Is war justified when it extends American power and brings democracy to other nations—or is peace a more worthy goal to pursue? America's citizens and leaders continue to struggle with these questions today.

But in the final years of the nineteenth century, Theodore Roosevelt was quite sure of the answers. "I should welcome almost any war," he told a friend, "for I think this country needs one."

Roosevelt had achieved national recognition for his role in the Spanish-American War in 1898, the first time that the U.S. military was significantly involved in a conflict outside of North America. In appreciation of his active campaigning for President William McKinley, Roosevelt had been rewarded with the position of assistant secretary of the U.S. Navy. In the pe-

Advocating means being in favor of something.

*To **annex** something means to take possession of it.*

riod immediately before the war's outbreak, Roosevelt had ensured that the U.S. fleet was prepared for action against the Spanish. At that point, the U.S. Navy consisted of only four first-class battleships. By the Great White Fleet's round-the-world voyage, the nation had twenty brand-new vessels.

Although McKinley had begun to shape the presidency to fit

Manifest Destiny

Political leaders of the 1840s used the phrase "Manifest Destiny" to describe the expansion of U.S. influence in the world. Many Americans and government leaders felt that the United States had a responsibility to spread the "boundaries of freedom" to others who would benefit from a democratic government. Not everyone was deemed worthy of U.S. involvement, only those who were determined to be capable of self-government. Native Americans and people of non-European origin were excluded.

Westward expansion was a logical outgrowth of the rapidly increasing U.S. population. Between 1800 and 1850, the population grew from 5 million to more than 23 million. The population had to live somewhere, and expansion into the western territories was a logical solution. Between 1820 and 1850, approximately 4 million people moved to the western territories, especially to farms and ranches. Frontier land was inexpensive—even free in some cases. Movement west also allowed for new business opportunities, which could lead to wealth, political power, and self-rule.

At the beginning of the twentieth century, many Americans—including Teddy Roosevelt—began to reason that Manifest Destiny should also apply to land beyond the North American continent.

Roosevelt's campaign speech

want to see our flag hauled down where it has been hauled up." In a letter to another friend, he expressed his desire to build a canal through Nicaragua, **annex** Hawaii, expel Spain from Cuba, and acquire the Danish Virgin Islands. Now that Roosevelt was President, he would have his chance to shape the new America he envisioned.

Increasing the abilities of the U.S. Navy was a large part of Roosevelt's plans. The ocean had fascinated him since he was young; he wrote his first book, *The Naval War of 1812*, when he was only twenty-three years old. In the book, he strongly advocated updating the U.S. fleet, which at that point was poorly maintained and not prepared for military confrontations.

Roosevelt's focus on foreign affairs was a natural transition from the administration of McKinley, which had already acquired the first overseas U.S. territory in the Spanish-American War. The Roosevelt administration, however, marked an even clearer departure from the previous post–Civil War administrations in which the political parties and the U.S. Congress generally played a larger role in national affairs than the President did. Roosevelt discovered the power of the "bully pulpit," as he termed it,

America's new place in the world, Roosevelt was eager to assume even greater responsibilities for the presidency and the country. As early as 1891, he had been ready for military involvement in Latin America, *advocating* war against Chile. In 1893, he wrote a friend: "I am a bit of a believer in the manifest destiny doctrine. I believe in more ships. I believe in ultimately driving every European power off this continent, and I don't

Domestic refers to the national, or home, level.

*An **agenda** is a plan.*

and used it skillfully to push his **domestic** and foreign **agenda**.

By the time Roosevelt was thrust into office by the assassination of President McKinley, the United States was more ready to play an active role on the world stage. America also had more room to operate because of the difficulties facing other imperial powers. Great Britain, which had been the dominant power around the world for so many years, was facing multiple foes. The French British ruled in Siam (now Thailand) and Africa. The Russians had their eyes on India and Constantinople. The Boers in South Africa had rebelled, and the Germans were confronting the British in Europe and Asia.

The Spanish-American War

The Assassination of William McKinley

The young man waited patiently in the eighty-two-degree weather to shake the hand of President William McKinley, the most popular president since Abraham Lincoln. The line moved quickly in the Temple of Music at the Pan-American Exposition in Buffalo, New York. Finally, it was the young man's turn to greet the President, but instead of shaking his hand, twenty-eight-year-old Leon Czolgosz shot the twenty-fifth President of the United States. As some members of the crowd and the President's entourage attended to the wounded leader, many members of the crowd attacked the shooter, beating him savagely. As the President's wound was being examined, it is reported that he told people around him, "Don't let them hurt him," referring to his assailant.

It was September 6, 1901. After surgery and at first a promising outlook, the President died of gangrene in the early morning of September 14.

Leon Czolgosz was born in Detroit to Polish immigrant parents. He had moved to Cleveland where he was often unemployed. He became an anarchist, someone who believed that all forms of government oppressed people and must be destroyed. He wanted to start at the top by killing the President of the United States.

Although Czolgosz eagerly confessed to the assassination, a plea of not guilty was entered for him as allowed by New York State law at the time. After a brief trial and an even briefer deliberation (thirty minutes), Czolgosz was found guilty. He was executed on October 29.

Now the British had to learn to live with the new power of the Americans. In the Spanish-American War, the British assisted the United States behind the scenes in preventing Spain from getting help from other European powers.

During the Roosevelt administration, the British also began to give up their aspirations for power in Central America.

Britain's power was waning—but America's was growing.

The British Empire

The reign of Elizabeth I saw the beginning of the spread of British influence throughout the world that would eventually become the British Empire. Her explorers traveled from the Arctic, to the deserts, to the Far East to lay claims on behalf of Britain.

The British Empire began as a competition between England and Spain, France, and Holland. They all wanted to acquire as much foreign land as possible for markets and as the source of products and raw materials. The English believed that a profitable balance of trade would bring them the money that would allow for even more expansion. And it worked, for a while. Britain would eventually establish trading companies in Turkey, Russia, and the East Indies, as well as explore and establish colonies in North America, Africa, and India. The seventeenth century brought even more colonization, and the influence of Britain grew.

The influence of the British began to weaken in the eighteenth and early nineteenth centuries. This was due in part to the abolition of slavery first in England and then in the rest of the British Empire. The influence of the once glorious British Empire weakened even more quickly after World War I, when other countries, such as the United States, rose to prominence in the world.

The British flag

Balboa

Two
THE PANAMA CANAL

On September 13, 1513, Vasco Nuñez de Balboa caught his first glimpse of the Pacific Ocean. Balboa had just dismantled his ships and dragged them through the jungle swamp of what was later named the Isthmus of Panama. His life would have been a lot easier if a waterway across the *isthmus* had been available.

The first person recorded to suggest a man-made waterway was Alvaro de Saavedra Ceron, a lieutenant of Hernando Cortez. Such a canal, Ceron said, would make the King of Spain the "master of the world." But any plans were abandoned when Philip II of Spain declared that such a project would be clearly against the will of God, because God had created the isthmus as a land barrier to shipping.

But the benefits of such a canal were obvious, and dreamers kept the idea alive. Without the canal, shippers had to circle around the stormy and dangerous Cape Horn at the southern tip of South America. This added thousands of miles to voyages to the Pacific.

*An **isthmus** is a narrow strip of land that joins two larger areas of land.*

Who Was Balboa?

Vasco Nuñez de Balboa was born in Spain in 1475. He sailed in 1500 with Rodrigo de Bastides from Spain to Colombia, South America, searching for treasure—especially pearls and gold—along the northern coastline of South America and the Gulf of Uraba. They found nothing of value, however, and their ship developed a serious leak. At last, they were forced to put aground on Hispanola (modern-day Cuba). With no money and no treasure, Balboa tried his hand at farming. He failed. With his dog Leoncio, Balboa stowed away on a ship sailing from Santo Domingo to San Sebastion in 1510. They arrived to find the village had been burned down. Undaunted, Balboa convinced others to go with him—and his dog—south. In 1511, Balboa and his followers established the first European settlement in South America, Santa Maria de la Antigua del Darien.

Balboa was not content with that accomplishment. He had tasted success and wanted more. So, in 1513, Balboa—and his dog—ventured overland through thick rainforests. Along the way, they killed many Indians and destroyed an Indian village. Despite the horrors they inflicted, Balboa will be remembered as the first European (well, along with his dog) to see the eastern part of the Pacific Ocean from a ridge along Darien. He and his party traveled to the Ocean and claimed it and all the land that touched it in the name of Spain. The explorers spent the next month traveling the Pacific Coast, conquering the Indians and stealing their gold.

In 1518, a friend of Balboa's, Arias de Avila, framed him for treason against Spain. Balboa was found guilty, and publicly beheaded in January 1519. There is no record as to what happened to his dog.

Panama

A ***penal colony*** is a prison at a remote location.

Seceded *means withdrew from.*

In 1779, Pierre-Andre Gargaz, a convict confined to a French ***penal colony*** at Toulon, gave a detailed plan for a Panama canal to Benjamin Franklin. Gargaz argued that canals in Panama and the Suez would promote trade and world peace. At the time, Franklin was serving as the U.S. ambassador to France, and was busy with the American efforts for independence. By the time Gargaz had been released from prison, the fighting had ended, and Franklin agreed to print Gargaz's canal plans on his private press.

Spain, meanwhile, had revisited the idea of a canal, and the Spanish national legislature passed a decree to build a canal across Nicaragua, using the San Juan River and Lake Nicaragua as the major part of the inter-oceanic route. When the Federal Republic of the United Provinces of Central America ***seceded*** from Mexico in 1825, the new government passed a law directing the canal to be built along the old Spanish route. Early in the 1800s, the United States considered proposals to join other countries to build the canal, but political and financial obstacles interfered. By the 1850s, however, expansionist feelings were dominant in

Ancon Hospital, Panama

Who Was Cortez?

Hernando Cortez was born in Medellin, Spain, in 1485, the son of minor nobility. When he was fourteen years old, he entered the University of Salamanca where he studied law. By 1501, he had decided that education wasn't for him, and spent the next few years trying to find his path in life. Not finding much luck in Spain, in 1504 he sailed for what is now the Dominican Republic to see what awaited him there. He joined an army commanded by Diego Velazquez in 1511, and participated in the conquest of Cuba. He was elected Mayor-Judge of Santiago.

Once word came that Mexico had been discovered, Cortez convinced Velazquez, now Cuba's governor, to back him in an exploration of the newly discovered land. Cortez and his men conquered the Mexican Aztecs in 1519, taking their leader, Montezuma II, captive and making him swear allegiance to Spain.

Hernando Cortez

Cortez returned to Spain in 1528, but his explorer's spirit would not rest. He returned to the North American continent in 1534 to explore California. There, he fought the pirates of Algiers (Africa) in 1541. Later that year, Cortez led a force against the Maya of southern Mexico. Finally, on December 2, 1547, Cortez died near Seville, Spain.

Construction of the Panama Canal

Andrew Johnson

Washington. The Clayton-Bulwer Treaty of 1850 provided the legal basis for a ***neutral*** canal to be built with support from both Britain and the United States.

The Panama Railroad Company ran its first train across the isthmus in 1855, and was soon paying great ***dividends*** to its ***stockholders***, fueling further interest in a canal—until the Civil War pushed it firmly off the agenda. After the war, President Andrew Johnson negotiated with Colombia, but the Senate rejected his efforts in 1869. President Grover Cleveland later added his blessing to a privately built and maintained canal, and in 1890, the Maritime Canal

Neutral *means not taking sides.*

Dividends *are stockholders' shares of a company's profits.*

Stockholders *are people who invest money in a company with the idea that they will eventually earn more than the amount they invested.*

Inaugurated means sworn into office.

Public relations refer to the promotion of a favorable image.

Ferdinand de Lesseps

Company of Nicaragua actually started construction work by the mouth of the San Juan River. The financial panic of 1893 shut it down, though.

Meanwhile, in 1880, a French group led by Ferdinand de Lesseps, famous for his work in creating the Suez Canal, put together a company to build a canal across the Isthmus of Panama. The company had thousands of investors, but Americans, fearing a French presence on the continent, were skeptical about his plans. Rutherford Hayes, who was President at the time, announced that no European nation would ever be allowed to control such a canal.

As things turned out, the French canal effort was doomed. The engineering plans were faulty, the business organization was corrupt, and the Central American jungle was a dangerous place to work. Floods, earthquakes, diseases, and accidents killed thousands of workers. At last, the French company abandoned its work and left everything behind. The machinery rusted away in the damp jungle, like ancient dinosaurs from another millennium.

All this time, young Theodore Roosevelt had kept a close eye on the issue. Long before he was President, he expressed his backing for an American-controlled canal across the isthmus. In 1894, while Roosevelt was serving as governor of New York, he wrote his friend Henry Cabot Lodge, "I do wish our Republicans would . . . build an oceanic canal with the money of Uncle Sam."

Shortly after Roosevelt was *inaugurated*, the Hay-Pauncefote Treaty was signed, which essentially gave the United States a free hand to construct and control a canal, providing that it was open to the merchant marine ships and warships of all nations. The new treaty replaced the Clayton-Bulwer Treaty, negotiated in 1850 between Great Britain and the United States. The Americans were ready to assume the leadership role in building the canal.

But despite centuries of wrangling over the issue, no one knew where exactly the canal would be built.

The two primary options were either through Nicaragua, the route favored earlier by Spain, or through Panama, which at that time was part of Colombia. The Nicaraguan route had the advantage of using the San Juan River and Lake Nicaragua, but a commission of U.S. Navy officers favored picking up where the French had left off in Panama. Roosevelt himself was familiar with the report on the canal and firmly favored the Panama route.

For two years, both sides bickered bitterly over the issue. The Nicaraguan route was favored by powerful Southern Democrats in the Senate, while the Republicans threw their weight behind the Panama option. The battle involved complicated legislative tactics and aggressive *public relations* campaigns on both sides. For example, when the volcano of Mt. Pelee blew up on the island of Martinique, Panama plan proponents argued that Nica-

Teddy Roosevelt's inauguration

ragua's volcanic activity made it unsuitable for construction of the canal. Nicaraguan postage stamps even displayed that country's landmark—the smoking volcano of Mt. Momotombo—and blocks of Nicaraguan stamps were sent to each senator so they would know how "dangerous" Nicaragua was.

When the French company dropped the asking price for its assets in Panama from $109 million to $40 million, the Panama option began to look still more attractive to Congress. There was just one problem: Colombia owned the Isthmus

Conspirators are people who join together to plot an illegal act.

of Panama, and it was asking for more money than America wanted to spend.

But Teddy Roosevelt refused to be discouraged. During the summer of 1903, he had a favorite game he called the "obstacle walk." He played it with his children and with guests to his home—and the only rule was the player must go up and over every obstacle, but never around it. Roosevelt was always the leader. His sister recalled seeing him approach

> an especially unpleasant-looking bathing-house with a very steep roof. . . . I can still see the sturdy body of the President of the United States hurling itself at the obstruction and with singular agility chinning himself to the top and sliding down the other side.

Roosevelt seemed to apply the same attitude to international affairs. He refused to let an obstacle stand in his way. Now, when it came to the Panama Canal, if Colombia was in the United States' way, he reasoned, then why not go in and create a new country that would be more agreeable?

During the fifty years Colombia had controlled the territory, revolutionary sentiment had already begun to fester. Now, Panamanians began to organize a conspiracy to secede. One of the *conspirators* angling for Panamanian independence was the general in charge of the Colombian forces on the isthmus. The conspirators met with the local superintendent of the Panama Railroad, an American. Planning for the revolution began in August of 1903, after the conspirators had been assured that they would receive military back-up from the U.S. government.

Map of canal

*A **sovereign power** is a governing body with complete authority over another.*

__Ratified__ means gave something formal approval.

*A **syndicate** is a group of businesspeople who combine to carry out a particular transaction or project.*

Roosevelt in Panama on machine

The events leading up to the revolution were complicated and secret. Panama hoped for more direct involvement on behalf of the United States, but they went ahead as planned. An American battleship, the *Nashville*, steamed south and pointed its guns at Colombia. The nation of Panama was born—and on November 6, 1903, the United States formally recognized the new government.

Twelve days later, Panama and the United States signed a treaty, and by December 7, 1903, America had been granted a ten-mile wide strip—the Canal Zone—across the new country "in perpetuity" (in other words, forever). Senator John Morgan, who had backed the Nicaraguan route, denounced the actions of the Roosevelt administration. In his protest, which filled thirty pages of the *Congressional Record,* the senator declared that Roosevelt performed a "caesarean operation" to take Panama "alive from the womb" of Colombia.

Predictably, there were also protests from abroad when the new treaty was made public. The Germans, for example, had been hoping to gain power in the Caribbean. They complained about yet another example of where the United States claimed special rights to act in the area.

Despite the complaints at home and abroad, the United States gained **sovereign power** within the Canal Zone. In return, the United States paid $10 million initially, and then a yearly rental of $250,000, beginning in 1912. The United States also had the right to add more territory for the operation of the canal if needed. And the United States would have the right to intervene in Panama to maintain or restore order for the security of the canal. Although many Panamanians were shocked by the terms of the treaty, the new republic **ratified** the treaty on December 2.

The *New York World* later charged that the whole canal deal had been arranged by a **syndicate** of Wall Street financiers, who manipulated the shares of the Panama Canal Company to make a $4 million profit on top of the $40 million that the U.S. government paid for its rights, property, and equipment on the isthmus. Roosevelt, outraged by the press report, sued the paper and its publisher, Joseph Pulitzer, for libel, but the suit was eventually dropped.

Roosevelt continued to defend his position, however. He wrote of the "habitual oppression" from which the United States had saved the Panamanians; he insisted that "our Government was bound by ever consideration of honor and humanity . . . to take exactly the steps that it took." The United States had a mandate from civilization to build the canal, he told Congress on January 4, 1904. "We did our duty, we did our duty by the people of Panama, we did our duty by ourselves," he wrote.

American relations with Colombia—and with the rest of Latin America—suffered as a consequence of Roosevelt's actions in Panama.

Panama hut

"I fear," said one American senator, "that we have become too large to be just." Today, the conflict between military intervention and peace, the understanding of the rights of power and democracy, continue to be issues as Americans seek to find their position in the world.

But in the 1900s, despite the bitter debate and condemnation over Panama, public opinion generally favored the treaty. During the presidential campaigns of that year, Democrats pledged that they would "contract the Panama Canal speedily, honesty and economically." Republicans, meanwhile, pointed out that "the great work of connecting the Pacific and Atlantic by a canal is at last begun, and it is due to the Republican Party."

And, during Roosevelt's second administration, the canal construction finally began. From the beginning, however, the work was plagued with the same problems the French had faced. Tropical heat, the jungle, and diseases were hard enemies to conquer. Nearly six thousand

men died, mostly from diseases like yellow fever and malaria. Enormous engineering problems had to be overcome.

But finally, in 1914, the Panama Canal was completed. Thanks to the United States, the Pacific and the Atlantic Oceans were finally linked.

A Panama native goes to market

Ship in canal

33

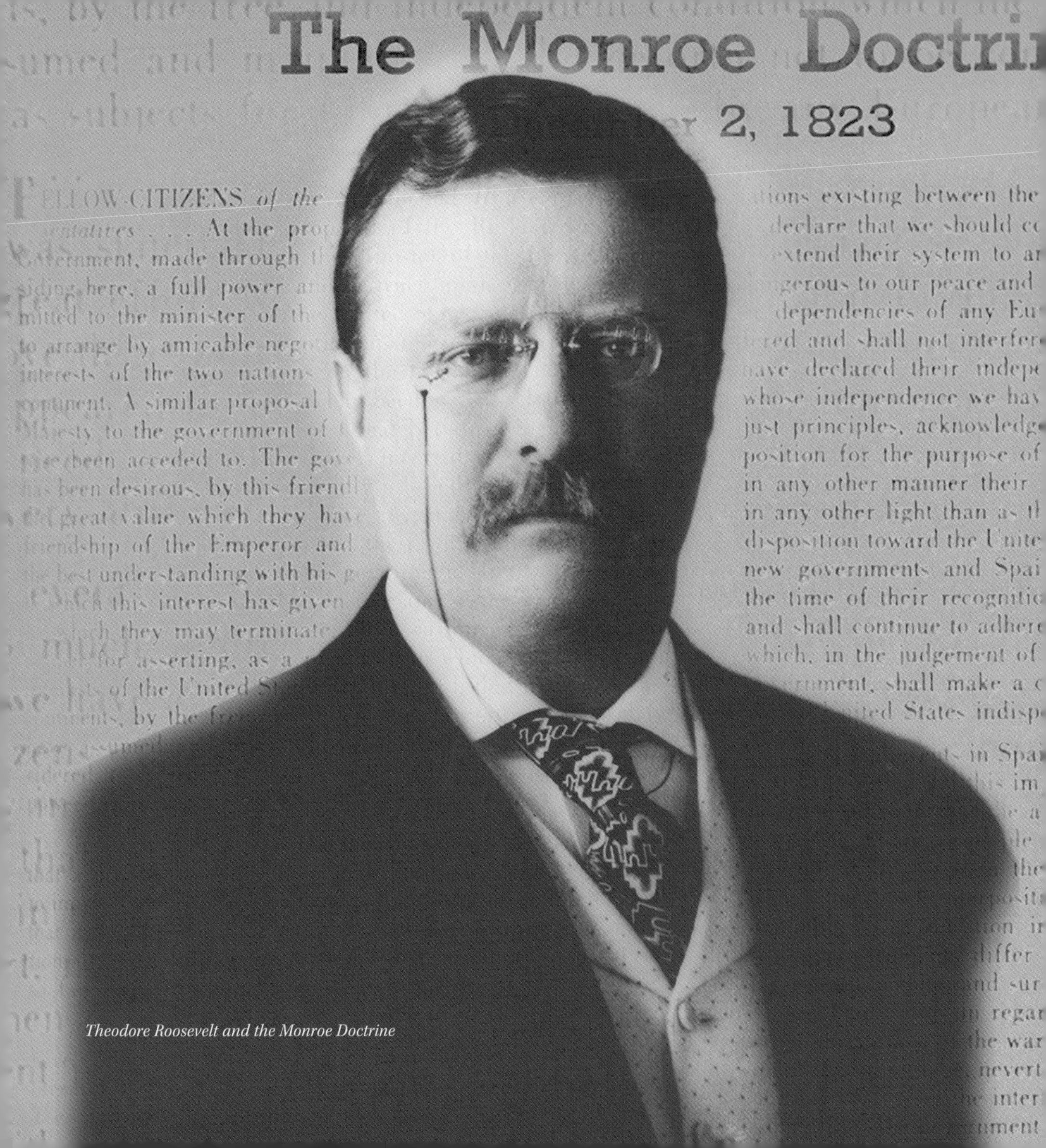

Theodore Roosevelt and the Monroe Doctrine

Three
THE ROOSEVELT COROLLARY

"Speak softly and carry a big stick."

This African proverb was Theodore Roosevelt's favorite motto. In reality, he seldom spoke softly—but he did carry a "big stick" when it came to his political interactions both at home and abroad. He believed he had good ideas—and he was willing to use whatever force necessary to bring those ideas to reality.

Teddy Roosevelt did great good while he was President. He helped pass pure food and drug laws; he found ways to control big corporations that acted as if they were above the law; and he set aside public lands as national parks. But Roosevelt also made Americans unpopular with some of their closest neighbors. He viewed Latin Americans as racially inferior, and he had no qualms about exerting American influence over their nations. He justified his actions with a new addition to the Monroe Doctrine, something he called the "Roosevelt Corollary."

The Monroe Doctrine was a ***unilateral*** declaration by U.S. President James Monroe that any European intervention in the Western Hemisphere would be viewed by the United States as a hostile act. The Roosevelt Corollary extended this policy even further; it stated in effect that the United States had a right to inter-

Unilateral means one-sided.

35

Chronic *means long-lasting or frequently recurring.*

Impotence *means powerlessness.*

Flagrant *means obvious and contrary to the standards of conduct or morality.*

Fiscal *has to do with financial affairs.*

A ***constitution*** *is a written set of the laws that govern a country.*

vene in order to maintain financial and social stability in its neighborhood. Roosevelt himself described the new corollary in his message to the U.S. Congress in 1904:

> All that this country desires is to see the neighboring countries stable, orderly and prosperous. Any country whose people conduct themselves well can count upon our hearty friendship. If a nation shows that it knows how to act with reasonable efficiency and decency in social and political matters, if it keeps order and pays its obligations, it need fear no interference from the United States. *Chronic* wrongdoing, or an ***impotence*** which results in a general loosening of the ties of civilized society, may in America, as elsewhere, ultimately require intervention by some civilized nation, and in the Western Hemisphere the adherence of the United States to the Monroe Doctrine may force the United States, however reluctantly, in ***flagrant*** cases of such wrongdoing or impotence, to the exercise of an international police power.

The reasoning behind the policy was that in order to keep Europeans out of the Western Hemisphere, specifically out of the area of the Caribbean, the United States had to correct the ***fiscal*** irresponsibility of the local states and keep political order by acting as an international police power. According to this theory, if the United States took over the task of ensuring Caribbean political stability and fiscal responsibility, European governments would have no legal basis to intervene.

The Roosevelt Corollary had complicated roots in the Dominican Republic.

General Ulises Heureaux was only thirty-seven years old in 1882

James Monroe

when he was inaugurated as president of the Dominican Republic. The son of former slaves, Heureaux was well educated, shrewd, and energetic. He enjoyed considerable popularity, and many Dominicans hoped his election—only the second peaceful transfer of power under the country's *constitution*—would bring their country some lasting stability.

Instead, Heureaux ruled as a dictator for sev-

enteen years. He was killed while trying desperately to raise money for his government from local merchants, assassinated by the son of a man he executed years earlier. His legacy of violence and disorder opened the door for the first application of the Roosevelt Corollary. The United States would intervene in the Dominican Republic's affairs for decades to come.

Heureaux's policies had led to a poor country with crushing debts to foreign creditors. The French government had attempted to get the funds owed to French businesses by anchoring the French Caribbean Fleet off the Dominican coast in a showdown with the government.

The United States had been deeply involved financially for years as well. The San Domingo Improvement Company (SDIC) was formed in New York in 1892 to essentially take over the Dominican foreign debt. In order to secure payment on this debt, the SDIC took control of the customs services of the country, which was the Dominican government's main source of income.

The U.S. government backed the SDIC because it believed that the company's control of Dominican finances would transform the

Dominican Republic into a *protectorate* of the United States, but the company never gained full control of the company's finances. In the end, Washington, Wall Street, and Heureaux used the SDIC to the detriment of investors and the Dominican economy. When the SDIC failed to make interest payments due on January 1, 1897, for example, the news of the default caused the value of Dominican securities to plummet. When it became clear that no more *gullible* European investors could be found, the Dominican government began printing money to finance itself.

The U.S. leaders weren't concerned with finances in the Dominican Republic simply because of the goodness of their hearts. Since the mid-1800s, the United States had been interested in acquiring naval access to Samana Bay, a key strategic harbor in the Caribbean. With the acquisition of Puerto Rico and Guantanamo Bay in Cuba in the Spanish-American War, however, Samana Bay lost some of its value. Heureaux's negotiating position with the United States deteriorated.

By the time Heureaux was killed in 1899, the Dominican Republic was deeply in debt to European bondholders, who requested assistance from their foreign ministries to recover debts owed to them. The country, which had hoped for some stability after the financial chaos of the Heureaux years, found itself ruled by a series of five provisional governments be-

tween 1899 and 1905. The SDIC, which supposedly had tried to improve the financial situation of the country, faced hostility from the local government after it dismissed all its Dominican employees from the customshouses, replacing them with foreigners. Americans in general were viewed unfavorably, as one U.S. Navy officer noted in a letter to his commander. The hostility, he wrote, "seems to be due somewhat to the influence and action of the American Improvement Company (SDIC), and also probably because the most valuable properties in the island belong to the Americans."

The company was expelled from the Dominican Republic in 1901 by the new president, Isidoro Jimenes, but the SDIC's relationship with the U.S. government remained strong. The U.S. government pressured the Dominican government to pay its debts to SDIC, without any examination of the origin of the debts. By January 1903, the Dominican government had agreed to pay the SDIC $4.5 million, allowing an international arbitration court to

Map of old Santa Domingo

*A **protectorate** is a country or region that is defended and controlled by a more powerful one.*

***Gullible** means easily tricked or deceived.*

Ulises Heureaux

Arbitration is a process for resolving conflicts between people or groups by using a neutral third party to make the judgment.

Unanimous means everyone is in complete agreement.

A tribunal is a group appointed to make a judgment.

set the guarantees that would be given by the country on the debt.

The SDIC's lawyer presented the case in the *arbitration* court, arguing that the instability of the Dominican government made payment of legal debts unlikely at best. He asked: "Is the plea that revolution and anarchy are the prevailing condition to prevent creditors from a reasonable and just enforcement of their debts? The answer must be no."

The arbitration judges were biased in the SDIC's favor. At least one was a personal friend of the lawyer, and others had various ties to the American government. So it wasn't too surprising when the panel's *unanimous* verdict was in favor of the SDIC. In the event that the Dominican government did not meet the payment schedule on its debt, the U.S. government itself would appoint a financial agent to take over up to four Dominican customshouses to collect funds on behalf of the SDIC. The *tribunal* also doubled the amount that the country had to pay each month.

The Dominican government failed to make its first payment under the award in September 1904. The Dominican president, Carlos Morales, said it would give up the customshouse at Puerto Plata only if the SDIC guaranteed the government a minimum income. Standing firm, the U.S. State Department refused to modify the ruling of the arbitration court, and the SDIC took control of the customshouse. As the British Consul on the scene described it, the takeover "required all the tact of the Government at Santo Domingo and the Governors of provinces and towns to keep down an armed demonstration of dissatisfaction."

In fact, the U.S. Navy had taken up position in Dominican wa-

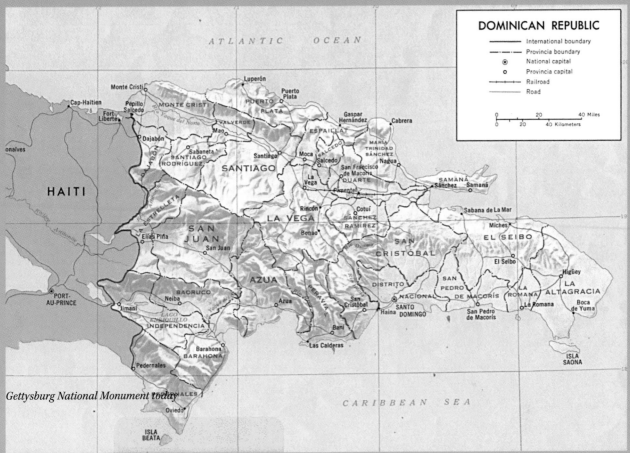

Gettysburg National Monument today

Map of the Dominican Republic

ters by January 1904—and their presence played a key role in curbing opposition to U.S. takeovers. The wisdom of the policy, however, was beginning to be questioned by many peo-

ple, ranging from naval officers to President Roosevelt himself. Admiral Charles Sigbee, for example, noted that at a cost of about $1.5 million a year to maintain the naval force in the

Dominican Republic flag

area, it would be cheaper for the United States to just pay the claims of the SDIC itself.

By the end of that year, the problems with the U.S. policy became obvious. The SDIC was not the only creditor owed money by the Dominican Republic. The country owed money to many creditors, but the government couldn't pay them because the SDIC seized all its income. As the Italian ambassador to Washington put it, "the United States must either let other countries follow its policy in the Dominican Republic, or it must treat all creditors equally." American sugar-planting interests also began to complain because the Dominican government was squeezing them to pay the SDIC debts. Was the U.S. government going to take sides in a conflict between two groups of Americans?

Confronted by these difficulties, President Roosevelt changed course, and the Roosevelt Corollary was born. The President changed U.S. policy in the Dominican Republic toward a more even-handed approach to that country's creditors. He declared the U.S. government's intervention was disinterested and wouldn't act

Samana Bay in the Dominican Republic

Marines at Santo Domingo

Political cartoon showing Roosevelt's political attitudes

to benefit any nation's investors. It was necessary, he said to "prove by our action that the world may trust in our good faith and may understand that this international duty will be performed by us within our own sphere, in the interests not merely of ourselves but of all other nations and with strict justice toward all."

For all its apparent wisdom, the policy also provided a rationale for America's intervention in the Caribbean area for years. And under the new policy in the Dominican Republic, the United States took over supervision of the customs collection in the country, reserving 55 percent of the receipts for the payment of foreign debts.

Over the next two years, the Roosevelt Corollary became the model for a strategy that used Washington-arranged loans for unstable countries that agreed to some level of financial supervision. The policy was aimed at keeping European warships out of the Caribbean; it also was an attempt to take control of foreign policy in an area where private American firms had financial interests.

Today, the Roosevelt Corollary lives on, reflected by policies of modern entities such as the International Monetary Fund (IMF).

The International Monetary Fund

The International Monetary Fund (IMF) is in the business of promoting monetary cooperation between countries. The IMF was proposed at a UN conference in July 1944. The governments participating in the meeting wanted to establish a framework for international economic cooperation that would prevent another Great Depression.

Currently, the IMF, headquartered in Washington, D.C., has 184 member countries. Financial assistance from the IMF is available to those countries if they are having problems financing their debt. Member countries can also receive technical assistance, as well as training from the IMF that will help them make their economy grow. The IMF also works with other organizations such as the World Bank to help reduce poverty around the world.

Help often comes with strings attached, however. The IMF monitors conditions—financial and political—in countries receiving aid. Many times that assistance is not renewed if the country has not lived up to its agreement.

Jose Santos Zelaya is portrayed on a Nicaraguan bill

Four
DOLLAR DIPLOMACY

On the east coast of Nicaragua, deep in the jungle, a revolution brewed. In 1909, it led to three years of political upheaval—and the presence of American troops in the country for decades. The policy that kept the troops there became known as "Dollar Diplomacy," an *ironic* term because military power was as much in evidence as was financial investment.

The causes of the strife in Nicaragua were as tangled and dense as the area's tropical forest. Jose Santos Zelaya had ruled Nicaragua as dictator since 1893, crushing any opposition to his power. Zelaya developed transportation and production networks in the country, but he also ensured that he and his associates profited from selling the country's natural resources.

The U.S. government did not view Zelaya favorably, both because of his anti-American attitude and because of his habit of interfering with the internal affairs of his neighbors. Perhaps most important for Americans, in 1909, Zelaya financed his country's national debt through loans from European banks. Under the

*Something that is **ironic** turns out differently from what was expected.*

Customs revenues refers to money that is paid on items entering a country.

Defaulted means failed to pay.

A consul is a government official working in another country promoting the interests of the official's home country and protecting its citizen-tourists.

Collateral means something used as security against a loan.

A customs commissioner is someone who oversees the importation of goods.

Nicaragua's jungle

terms of the loan agreement, the Europeans got control over ***customs revenues*** and had the right to intervene directly if Nicaragua ***defaulted*** on its debts.

In October 1909, a group of Nicaraguans, with funding from some local Americans and their associates in the United States, were successful in seizing the east coast of the country. But Zelaya thwarted a simultaneous uprising in the interior, arresting its leaders. He also captured two Americans while they allegedly were attempting to blow up a troop ship. Despite the pleas of the American ***consul***, Zelaya ordered them shot.

The U.S. government responded to the executions by cutting formal ties with the Nicaraguan government; the United States published a formal protest that Zelaya's regime was a "blot upon the history of Nicaragua." Eventually, a rebellion against the government succeeded, and Adolfo Diaz, who had once worked as a bookkeeper for an American mining company in Nicaragua, was installed as president.

Diaz received U.S. backing on the condition that Nicaragua look to the United States, rather than Europe, if it needed financial help. After Diaz's inauguration, U.S. Secretary of State Philander Knox signed an agreement with the Nicaraguan minister to Washington, Salvador Castrillo, that would essentially turn the country into a protectorate of the United States. For its part, the United States refunded the Nicaraguan debt with an American loan. As in the Dominican Republic, Nicaragua pledged its customs receipts as ***collateral***, with a ***customs commissioner*** approved by the American government.

Philander Knox

Nationalists are people who desire political independence and are extremely loyal and devoted to a nation.

A *flotilla* is a naval unit consisting of two squadrons of small warships.

Revenue refers to government income from all sources.

William Howard Taft

Nicaragua defaulted on its European debt less than a month after signing the agreement with the United States, but the U.S. Department of State persuaded American bankers to provide a short-term loan to fund the debt. To gain control of the country's income, the Americans took control of the Nicaraguan customshouse.

In time, U.S. domination fed resentment among Nicaraguans. In July 1912, *nationalists* under the direction of former president Zaleya attacked Managua. In response, the United

States sent a *flotilla* of eight American warships with 2,500 Marines and sailors. After the revolt was crushed, 100 Marines stayed to guard the Americans in Nicaragua, and an American warship remained off the coast. In 1913, Diaz, who now depended on the United States to stay in power, negotiated a new treaty with the United States to underwrite loans to Nicaragua. The two countries signed a treaty giving the United States naval bases in the country and the right to build and operate a canal across Nicaragua in return for a $3 million payment. The treaty was not ratified until 1916, when U.S. warships again came patrolling Nicaraguan waters.

Nicaragua was not the only nation that endured the pressure of "Dollar Diplomacy." During the Taft administration, the United States took over tax col-lection in other Central American countries as well. The U.S. State Department rationalized that European creditors might take control of the customshouses in these other countries in order to secure their debts. This would give Europe a foothold in the region. To avoid this, the United States attempted to put the finances of these countries in order.

In Honduras, for example, Secretary of State Knox offered to reorganize the country's finances, and he assisted in negotiating an agreement between the government and its creditors. The country owed more than $120 million in 1909, and its annual *revenue* was about $1.65 million. Because many of these debts were to European bankers who knew their governments were not eager for a fight with the United States, the creditors agreed to be paid a small fraction of what they were owed. The Honduran government, however, couldn't even pay this small

A 1913 warship

Provisional means temporary.

Indemnity means compensation paid for loss or damage.

amount, and so the Honduran customshouses came under U.S. control.

The situation in Honduras became more complicated in 1911 when a band of rebels, led by Manuel Bonilla and funded by the United Fruit Company, tried to topple President Miguel Davila. If the United States took over the customs services, the tax concessions to the big American-owned fruit company would be voided.

After it became clear that Bonilla and his rebels could prevail, the United States attempted to find a solution. Seeing the very real possibility of a rebel victory, the United States selected Francisco Bertrand, a candidate suggested by the revolutionaries, who was then duly elected as the *provisional* president until the next election.

Bonilla, however, had great influence over the new president, and did not favor the treaty the previous administration had signed. Instead, Bonilla attempted to find new sources to finance his country's debt. The United Fruit Company even suggested paying up to $50,000 a year toward the debt, in return for wharf and a railroad. The United States, however, was cool to this idea, and the proposal died a quiet death.

Despite what happened in Honduras, Knox attempted to reach similar agreements with Costa Rica and Guatemala. Both countries, however, refused to surrender control of their customshouses.

Although the involvement of U.S. bankers did not lead to any large military presence in either Costa Rica or Guatemala, the loans the Haitian government made with Americans in 1910 led to

United Fruit Company docks

Stock certificate for United Fruit Company

U.S. troops occupying the country five years later.

Haiti's history was quite different than the rest of the nations in the Caribbean. A former colony of France, Haiti was created by former slaves who revolted in 1791 and declared their country's independence in 1804. France recognized the nation's independence, in return for a large *indemnity*, but the United States did not acknowledge Haiti until 1862. The Haitians

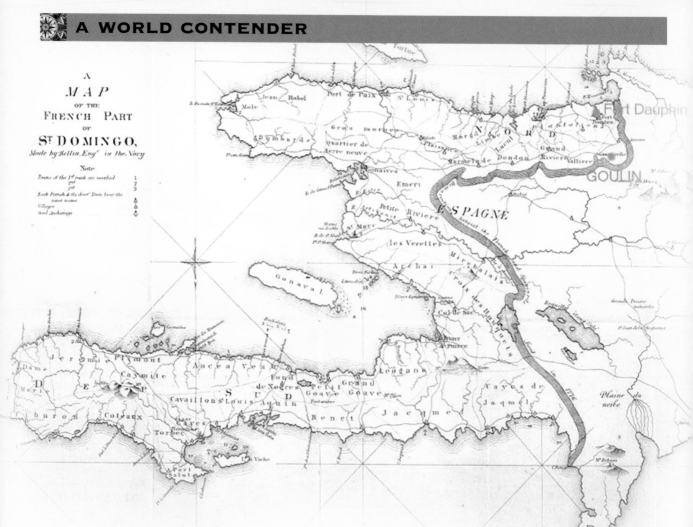

themselves resisted outside influences, and for years, foreigners were forbidden by law to own land in the country.

By 1900, many foreigners, primarily Germans and French, lived in Haiti's capital of Port au Prince. The principal market for Haitian coffee was France, and French bankers had loaned the country money in 1875 and 1896. The Germans were mostly merchants, but the most important group of Germans owned some of the local utilities and the PCS Railroad, which ran from Port au Prince into the interior.

When the French-controlled National Bank tried to persuade the Haitian government to restore the treasury service in return for financial assistance, the U.S. minister to Haiti was alarmed. He thought the agreement, which would give up customs collections to the French, would be "contrary to the spirit of the Monroe Doctrine," and he pushed for other arrangements within Haiti's financial world. A ***coup*** financed by the Germans, who opposed greater American economic involvement, toppled the government, however, before any agreements could be reached. Just one year after that coup, an explosion at the presidential palace killed the new president. A new government was organized a month later and accepted greater American involvement.

The policy of "Dollar Diplomacy" was most aggressively practiced in the Caribbean, but it did not have geographic limits. Instead, it spread far to the east. President William Taft's inaugural address refers to an issue where this policy would soon be applied:

*A **coup** is sudden, and often extremely violent, overthrow of a ruling body.*

> In the international controversies that are likely to arise in the Orient growing out of the question of the open door and other issues, the United States can maintain her interests intact and can secure respect for her just demands. She will not be able to do so, however, if it is understood that she never intends to back up her assertion of right and her defense of her interest by anything but mere verbal protest and diplomatic note.

By May of that year, the Chinese government agreed with German, British, and French bankers for a loan to construct the Hukuang railways, including lines from Hankow to Szech and from Hankow to Canton. A group of American bankers, headed by J. P.

William Taft seated

Haiti's flag

Morgan, organized immediately to finance any railroad concessions that Americans could get from the Chinese government. The bankers wanted to be admitted into the international group of bankers who would float the loan for the railroad. Secretary Knox asked the Chinese government to consider the Americans. Four days later, the Chinese government signed an agreement with German, British, and French bankers.

The Chinese government was reluctant to reopen negotiations, despite the pressure applied by the U.S. Department of State. Finally, President Taft sent a personal message to

Prince Chun, regent of the Chinese Empire, stating that he was "disturbed at the reports that there is a certain prejudiced opposition to your Government's arranging for equal participation by American capital in the present railway loan." Given the presidential pressure, the American group of bankers was admitted into the agreement.

But the Americans were looking for other opportunities besides railroad financing. When the Chinese government faced a financial crisis, a plan for loaning $50 million was suggested. While the Americans originally hoped to manage this plan alone, they soon agreed to work

J. P. Morgan

John Pierpont Morgan

To say that John Pierpont Morgan had a privileged life would be an understatement. He was born April 17, 1837, into a wealthy family. He had the finest of education—first at the English High School in Boston and then at the University of Göttingen. After college, he worked as a banker and eventually became a lawyer. He joined his father's banking house, J. S. Morgan & Co., now known as J. P. Morgan & Co., and helped it become one of the most influential banks in the world.

The world's first billion-dollar corporation, U.S. Steel, was financed by J. P. Morgan & Co. They even bailed out the U.S. Treasury with $62 million in gold! When J. P. Morgan & Co. bought the Leyland line of steamships and some British lines, the International Mercantile Marine Co. was created. The company is perhaps best known for one of the world's most famous shipping disasters. The company owned the *Titanic*.

Morgan's interests went beyond banking. He was prominent in the Episcopal Church, was an expert yachtsman (his boat *Columbia* won the America's Cup in 1899 and 1901), and he was an avid collector of books and art objects. Morgan also served as president of the Metropolitan Museum of Art, the "Met," in New York City. He died on March 31, 1913.

Stabilization of the currency has to do with maintaining the value of a country's monetary unit.

Stipulated means specified as a condition of something.

with British, French, and German bankers. The loan for about $50 million provided funds for promotion of Chinese industry and ***stabilization of the currency***. The interest rate was five percent and the loan period was forty years. For security, the lenders accepted the rights to taxes on tobacco, production, consumption, and salt. China couldn't decrease or abolish these taxes without the bankers' permission.

The Chinese government, however, was overthrown in a revolution in 1911, and the new government informed its bankers that Russian and Japanese bankers should be included in a new consortium. After long negotiations, a draft agreement was signed in 1913, which ***stipulated*** that non-Chinese would be employed in important administrative posts and as tax collectors and customs supervisors.

But 1913 brought a change of power in Washington as well, when the administration of President Woodrow Wilson took office. In a statement two weeks after his inauguration, Wilson withdrew support for the American group of bankers led by J. P. Morgan & Co. The terms forced on the Chinese government were unfair, Wilson said, and his government would not be party to enforcing them. He said:

> The responsibility on the part of our government implied in the encouragement of a loan thus secured and administered is plain enough and is obnoxious to the principles upon which the government of our people rests.

With this change in policy, the American banking group withdrew from the Six Power Consortium, as it was known. The start of

Bond certificate for the Hukuang Railway

World War I in 1914 slowed Americans' eager search for profits in this areas, but the principals of "Dollar Diplomacy" retained an informal power over the way America looked at the rest of the world.

Woodrow Wilson

General John Pershing

Five
PRESIDENT WILSON'S FOREIGN POLICIES

Among the military actions taken by the U.S. government over the years, it's hard to find a more futile mission than that of General John Pershing in Mexico. Sent by President Woodrow Wilson to find Pancho Villa in 1916, Pershing and his 11,000 soldiers wandered around Mexico for three months, searching for the rebel leader.

Pershing never did find Villa, but his soldiers killed dozens of other Mexicans and created even deeper hostility toward the Americans. The American general's mission, however, was just the capstone in an American policy toward Mexico that was so counterproductive it achieved none of its objectives.

During the Mexican-American War that was fought from 1846 to 1848, the United States had seized roughly one-third of Mexico's territory. But by the end of the nineteenth century, relations had become stable between the two neighboring nations. Porfirio Diaz had led Mexico since 1877, and he offered generous concessions to foreign business interests—but his policies were less helpful for common Mexicans. Instead, he ruthlessly oppressed Mexico's native tribes, while he allowed Americans to take control of thousands of acres of Mexican land. In order to support his government, Diaz borrowed liberally, and by the end of his administration, almost two-thirds of Mexico's wealth was pledged to foreigners either through con-

Indigenous means native born.

Reneging means not following through on something; breaking a promise.

Francisco Madero

cessions or as collateral for loans.

Diaz's regime was also notoriously corrupt, and what rewards came from development of the country's resources were funneled to his supporters. In 1910, a revolution broke out among the mestizo (mixed *indigenous* and white) population. The middle class joined the revolution during the following year, and the president fled the country for France.

Constitutionalists, as the revolutionaries called themselves, installed Francisco Madero, a politically moderate lawyer, as president. The movement, however, was soon split between radicals who wanted to completely change the system that Diaz had established, the army, and members of the old regime, who had a vested interest in the old system.

The foreign investors in Mexico watched the changes anxiously, because they feared losing their profitable concessions. Some members of the Constitutionalists proposed *reneging* on the concessions to the oil and mining companies, and raising taxes on the foreigners. Plans for redistribution of land of the plantation owners were also proposed.

The local representatives of a British oil company met with opponents to the Madero regime, who included soldiers discouraged by the president's perceived hostility to the armed forces. The plotters chose Victoriano Huerta, one of Diaz's respected generals, to lead the coup. In February 1913, troops loyal to Huerta surrounded the presidential palace in Mexico City and murdered Madero.

When President Wilson took office three weeks later, the United States had still not recognized the Huerta government, and

Wilson continued this policy of nonrecognition of the Huerta government, despite the fact that Huerta had effectively taken control of Mexico. In Wilson's eyes, the Constitutionalists had the best chance of establishing a democratic rule in Mexico, so he was especially outraged when he learned that the U.S. minister to Mexico had assisted the coup. The president replaced that ambassador with John Lind, a former Democratic governor of Minnesota.

Simply replacing the minister did not signify recognition of Huerta's administration. Lind carried a proposal for a nationwide election between the Huerta government and the opposition members of the Constitutionalists. This proposal was rejected, but for a time it appeared that Huerta would not be seizing dictatorial control.

Huerta dashed those hopes in October 1913, however, when he arrested 110 supporters of the former president and declared a military dictatorship. Wilson demanded that the Department of State be firm in opposing the new dictatorship. Wilson suspected that Europeans were working with Huerta in order to continue their profitable concessions. Such interference, Wilson declared in a famous speech

Porfirio Diaz

at Mobile, Alabama, on October 27, was unacceptable and unfair. In his speech, Wilson proclaimed:

> The Latin American States have had harder bargains driven with them in the matter of loans than any other peoples in the world. Interest has been exacted of them that was not exacted of anybody else, because the risk was said to be greater; and then securities were taken that destroyed the risk—an admirable arrangement for those who were forcing the terms!

Wilson's *emissary* subsequently did meet with a Venustiano Carranza, leader of the Constitutionists, but Carranza said the Mexicans didn't need American guidance in democracy and didn't need the support of the Americans. Carranza did, however, want the right to buy arms and the recognition as Mexico's legitimate government.

Although Wilson was unwilling to assist the rebels under these terms at first, the arms *embargo* against Mexico was eventually lifted in February 1914. The Americans themselves invaded Mexico in April of that year after what might have been just a diplomatic incident expanded into an "affair of honor."

En route to American Field Headquarters in Mexico

After some U.S. Navy personnel were arrested in Tampico, Mexico, the commander of the American squadron anchored off Vera Cruz demanded a twenty-one-gun salute from the Mexicans. The Mexican government refused, noting that the American government didn't even recognize the Mexican government. Wilson ordered the U.S. Navy to land in Vera Cruz and occupy the city, which they did by April 23. The battle for control, however, cost the lives of 126 Mexicans and nineteen Americans. It had also stirred domestic and international opposition.

The Americans eventually agreed to *mediation*, but while the talks continued, the Constitutionalists drove Huerta from office. Wilson still was angry at Carranza, however, for refusing to take direction from the Americans, and the Americans threw their support to Pancho Villa, a former Contitutionalist general who was feuding with Carranza. Villa linked up with Emiliano Zapata, a peasant leader who had been warring with the central government for years.

*An **emissary** is someone who represents a government on a particular mission.*

*An **embargo** is a government restriction on trade with another country.*

***Mediation** means the intervention by a third party between two disputing parties with the intention of helping them reach an agreement.*

Headquarters of American forces in Colonia Duban, Mexico

Revolutionary Heroes

Pancho Villa and Emiliano Zapata are two of the most beloved of Mexican revolutionary heroes.

Doroteo Arango was born in San Juan del Río, Durango, Mexico, in either 1877 or 1879—sources vary. He lived there until he was sixteen, when he killed a man who had raped his sister. No one knows for certain where he spent the next four or five years, but when he resurfaced he had become Francisco Villa. He moved north to Chihuahua, where he worked as a miner and as a "wholesale meat-seller" (the official Mexican government's term for someone who sells stolen cattle). Mining soon became boring for Villa, and he started robbing banks. The Mexican government was still looking for him for the murder committed years before and for selling stolen livestock.

Villa and his gang were well established by the early 1900s. Although they were being sought by authorities for a variety of crimes, the poor began to look at him as a hero. After all, it took skill to evade police capture. Then, in 1910, Villa's gang came down from the Sierras to fight alongside Francisco Madero's forces in the Mexican revolution.

Many Americans came to Mexico to fight beside the legendary Pancho Villa. His reputation grew in the United States, and Hollywood filmmakers went to northern Mexico to film his battles, many of them staged for the benefit of the camera. The media who recorded Villa saw a man who ordered executions, often for no apparent reason, while breaking up large ranches and giving them to widows and orphans of the soldiers serving with him.

Pancho Villa was assassinated in 1923 while returning from an ordinary trip to the bank in Chihuahua.

Emiliano Zapata was born in San Miguel Anencuilco, Morelos, on August 8, 1879. By 1909 he had been elected as a leader in his village. He began recruiting an army from among the men in his and surrounding villages even before the Mexican revolution had begun. In 1910, he and his army overthrew Mexican dictator Porfirio Díaz. Although Díaz was no longer in power, Zapata was not happy with the new government of Francisco Madero. He and his Liberation Army of the South fought troops led by Victoriano Huerta. Huerta was deposed in 1914.

Zapata had a plan, which he had devised in 1911. His plan, the "Plan de Ayala," called for the land, forests, and water to be returned to the people from whom they had been taken. "Tierra y libertad"—land and liberty—was their battle cry.

Over the years, Zapata did not back down. He fought for the rights of the people until April 10, 1919, when he was gunned down on the way to a meeting with government troops. Although his army continued to fight, the redistribution of land did not happen until years later with the presidency of Lázaro Cárdenas.

Pancho Villa and others

By now, America was busy with the building tension in Europe. Wilson wanted to avoid an unnecessary military conflict with Mexico, so he declared the United States neutral in the Mexican civil war. But when the United States recognized the Carranza government in October, Villa felt betrayed, and on March 9, 1916, the rebel leader crossed into the United States, killing nineteen Americans. On March 15, General Pershing began his quest in search of the elusive Mexican rebel.

American forces never found Villa, but the search to find him escalated into a large-scale military operation with more than 11,000 American soldiers inside Mexico. The U.S. National Guard patrolled the Mexico-U.S. border, and American warships sailed outside ports on the east and west coasts of Mexico.

Carranza at first had agreed to a U.S. search party, but not to the military action that ensued. He demanded that the U.S. troops leave, and on July 4, 1916, the United States agreed to mediation. The United States, however, refused to withdraw its troops without protections in place for its oil and mining interests and a promise to lower taxes on U.S. citizens in Mexico. The

Carranza government would not agree to this, and talks between the two governments broke down.

Wilson was reelected in 1916, and by the first months in his administration a war with Germany looked likely. The Mexicans in the meantime had elected Carranza president under the new constitution. The United States finally recognized his government on March 13, 1917.

Wilson's policy in Mexico, ineffective as it was in obtaining his goals, had a substantial impact. Within Mexico, it created distrust and resentment of the country's northern neighbor for more than a generation. For its part, the Huerta regime impressed on Wilson the evils of tyranny and perhaps fostered his insistence on imposing political stability in the Caribbean. Clearly, Mexico dominated Wilson's attention in the area, and he delegated most of the other matters in the Caribbean area to the State Department.

Things were not quiet in the Caribbean. In March 1913, instability in the Dominican Republic caught the attention of the Wilson administration, when the provisional president of the country resigned. A provisional president, Jose Bordas Valdes, was selected, but he did not have the support of local leaders. These leaders, in fact, held the real power in the country, and one local strongman, Desiderio Arias, took control of several provinces and extorted money from the Dominican government. After Arias was suspected of taking control of an important railway line in the country, the U.S.S. *Des Moines* was ordered to the Dominican city of Puerto Plata, and the U.S. government issued a statement to discourage "any and all insurrectionary methods."

The United States attempted to mediate between the feuding factions, and the opposition parties laid down their arms in October. An election was held under the supervision of U.S. observers, but the Dominican Republic's finances, always shaky, did not benefit from this exercise in democracy. By 1914, the government was facing about $1 million in claims, including $386,000 in back salaries. The Americans agreed to back $1.6 million in bond sales— on the condition that outside financial experts advise the government.

The U.S.S. Des Moines

*A **comptroller** is someone who oversees an organization's finances.*

Arias, meanwhile, continued to cause problems for the government, and the U.S. minister suggested the Dominican president should "eliminate Arias and his gang" by declaring Arias an outlaw. Other government opponents were angry because the new Dominican government did not pass a promised electoral reform law. The opponents blamed both the United States and the Dominican administration. By the end of May, the opposition parties had formed a coalition against President Bordas, and the Haitian government was helping the rebels obtain ammunition and weapons.

To address the county's problems, the United States presented the "Wilson Plan," which included provisions for U.S.-supervised elections, the appointment of a U.S. **comptroller** as a financial advisor to the Dominican government, the appointment of an American-chosen director of public works for the Dominican government, and the creation of a Dominican national guard under the command of the U.S. military.

Juan Isidro Jimenez was elected president under the plan, but he had only weak control of the country. In the summer of 1915, Jimenez, who was feeble and elderly, had a breakdown and gave control of the government to his bitterly divided cabinet. After a small uprising, the American owners of several sugar plantations requested government protection.

The Wilson administration had appointed Robert Lansing as the new secretary of state in June 1915, and he was more willing to get involved in other nations' affairs than his predecessor had been. He warned the Dominican government that it had to comply

Map of Central America and the Caribbean

Building of the Panama Canal

with a 1907 treaty, under which it pledged not to increase its debt without the permission of the United States.

The U.S. government continued to offer armed support to the Jimenez administration, but that didn't help, and the Dominican congress *impeached* Jimenez in April 1916. The United States then announced it would invade the country to preserve public order and the Jimenez administration, and U.S. Marines landed on May 5. On November 29, the United States proclaimed its occupation, creating a military government that lasted until September 1924.

Meanwhile, Wilson had also inherited a situation not of his choosing in Panama. On the one hand, the canal was almost finished when Wilson was elected president for the first time. But controversy surrounding the project remained. The British objected to the law passed by Congress in 1912 exempting U.S. ships from toll charges. The Hay-Pauncefote Treaty of 1900, they charged, provided that the canal would be open to British and American vessels under equal treatment.

When this objection was raised, the canal wasn't yet open, and the Taft administration just ignored the issue. But Wilson had to face the problem, and after meeting with the officials who had negotiated the Hay-Pauncefote Treaty, he decided to ask Congress to repeal the toll exemption. Within the United States, the argument on the issue was bitter. Many Americans favored keeping the exemption, and

saw Wilson as giving in too easily to the demands of Great Britain. But in his 1914 message to Congress on the issue, Wilson argued:

> Whatever may be our own differences of opinion concerning this much debated measure, its meaning is not debated outside the United States. We are too big, too powerful, too self-respecting a nation to interpret with too strained or refined a reading the words of our own promise just because we have power enough to give us leave to read them as we please.

After a vigorous debate within Congress, repeal of the toll exemption passed, and since the canal's opening, U.S. ships have paid the same tolls as the ships of all others passing through the Panama Canal.

Wilson's administration also saw the completion of the long-negotiated purchase of the Virgin Islands from Denmark. Since President Abraham Lincoln's administration, the United States had sought ownership of the islands of St. Thomas, St. John, St.

Impeached means to bring charges against an elected official with the ultimate purpose being his or her removal from office.

73

Martial law is the control and policing of a civilian population by military force according to military rules.

Croix, and about fifty smaller islands with a total area of about 150 square miles. Settled by Danes who came to St. Thomas in 1666, they were subsequently populated by the slaves who worked on plantations.

The United States had wanted the islands for their strategic value, and in 1866, America offered Denmark $5 million for the islands. The negotiations were tied up between political conflicts between President Andrew Johnson and the U.S. Congress, however, and the matter was ignored for several administrations. But as U.S. power grew at the end of the nineteenth century, the U.S. government again considered the matter, but several attempts to buy the island fell through. Then in 1915, the matter suddenly became more urgent. The outbreak of World War I raised the strategic value of the islands, and the U.S. government feared that Germany might seize Denmark and Danish possessions in the Caribbean.

Denmark also feared invasion by Germany, and it offered to sell the islands to the United States for $30 million. Many Danes opposed the sale on several grounds. For one, Danish women had the right to vote, but American women did not. Danes argued that the sale of the islands would mean that women living there would lose rights. The opponents also said the descendants of slaves on the islands did not suffer from racism the same way as African Americans living in the United States did at the time. From the Danes' perspective, America did not offer the freedom and protection of individual rights that their own nation did.

These objections were overcome, however, and in August 1916, the sale was completed in exchange for $25 million from the United States. The fears of some opponents, however, were not un-

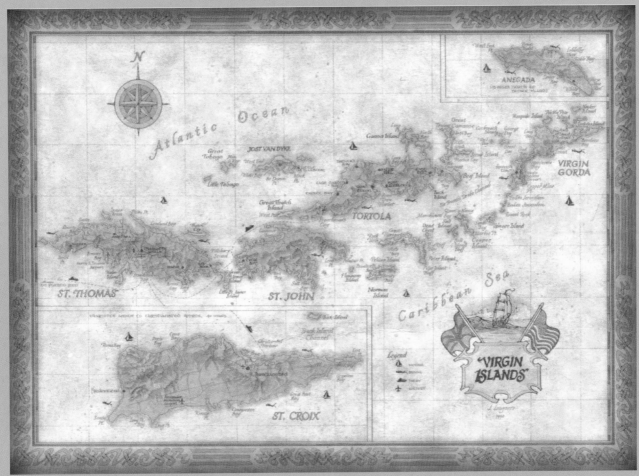

The Virgin Islands

founded. The United States established ***martial law*** on the islands in 1917 as a temporary measure, but it continued after World War I ended. Under the military dictatorship established by the United States, American sailors and Marines stationed on the island brutally attacked natives, but the Virgin Islands police had no power to arrest the attackers. The military

Libel *is a false and malicious published statement that damages someone's reputation.*

An *archipelago* *is a group of islands.*

Autonomous *means self-governing; self-sufficient.*

rule on the islands also suppressed the free press, charging editors who criticized the military rule with criminal *libel*.

Even as America took a firm grip on the Virgin Islands, on the other side of the globe, the Wilson administration was loosening its control over the Philippines, a territory acquired during the Spanish-American War. In 1913, Wilson appointed five Filipinos to the Philippine Commission, giving it a Filipino majority for the first time. Wilson also appointed Francis Burton to administer the Philippines. Burton attempted to give Filipinos more say in running their country.

A major step in this direction was taken with the passage of the Jones Act of 1916, which stated the desire to give the Philippines independence as soon as a stable government was in place. The law brought the legislative branch of the Philippines under Filipino control, although the executive branch was still under the control of a governor appointed by the U.S. President.

While the law was a step to independence for much of the Philippines, the Jones Act did not transfer responsibility for the Muslim areas within the *archipelago*, which had been traditionally *autonomous*. Because of this, the Muslims saw the Jones Act as a threat because they feared domination by the Christians. The new law also did not recognize Muslim customs and institutions, but it remained the basic legislation for administering the Philippines until the U.S. Congress passed new legislation in 1934.

Flag of the Philippines

President Wilson brought about many reforms within the United States. The Federal Trade Commission was created, and the Clayton Antitrust Act was passed, both of which were intended to control unfair and restrictive business practices. But Wilson also felt that America belonged to white people; under his administration the federal government became segregated, and African Americans lost government jobs.

This same attitude was reflected in Wilson's actions toward Latin America and other international affairs. Teddy Roosevelt may have carried a big stick—but Wilson carried out Roosevelt's legacy by acting like a superior big brother to non-white nations. From Wilson's perspective, America always knew best—and it had the right to exert its will over other "inferior" nations.

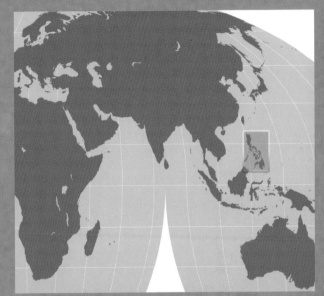

The Phillipines

Muslims in the Philippines

Islam has a long history in the Philippines. Arab merchants and Islamic missionaries brought Islam to the Philippine Islands in 1210, even before Catholicism, the country's most-practiced religion. Today, approximately five percent of the country's population is Muslim.

Police seize the young man who assassinated the archduke.

Six
WORLD WAR I

When a nineteen-year-old Serbian student assassinated Austrian Archduke Franz Ferdinand on June 28, 1914, in the Bosnian capital of Sarjevo, no one could have foretold, the bloodshed that would follow. That murder prompted a chain of events that led to World War I, a conflict that claimed the lives of millions of people and shook apart empires.

But while the conflict's scope still seems so out of proportion to its small beginning, in some ways the war was just the culmination of years of establishing military alliances. Once Austria issued its harsh demands on Serbia in retribution for the archduke's murder, Russia became involved. Germany backed Austria, but France had a defense pact with Russia. And the British had a defense pact with France. Like a game of dominoes, the nations were lined up to fall toward war. The assassination of the archduke was the first domino to fall, the one leading to the tumbling of all others.

Americans, meanwhile, generally viewed the beginnings of the conflict with a mixture of bewilderment and detachment. Few remembered the last major war in Europe in 1871, and the causes of this conflict seemed far away and hard to understand.

President Woodrow Wilson's first reaction was to declare strict neutrality for the United States. On August 1, 1914, the President urged

*To be **impartial** means to not take sides.*

__Autocratic__ means governed by a ruler with unlimited power.

__Civil liberties__ are basic rights guaranteed to individual citizens by law—for example, the freedoms of speech and religion.

*An **ultimatum** is a demand accompanied by a threat of penalty if the demand is not met.*

Americans to be ***impartial***, holding out hope that the nation might be able to help find a resolution to the conflict.

But neutrality was a difficult position for Americans, and for Wilson himself. For one thing, Wilson couldn't help but sympathize with the British. He admired British culture and British representative government, while Wilson considered that Germany exemplified ***autocratic*** government. Also, Germany was the nation that had declared war on France and Russia, and invaded neutral Belgium.

The American public, naturally, held mixed opinions about the growing conflict in Europe. The United States is a nation of immigrants, many of whose ancestors came from the nations fighting in the conflict. While the descendants of English and French naturally wanted to see the United States favor their homelands, other immigrant groups, such as the Irish, urged the United States to stay clear of the conflict.

Wilson was also identified with the Progressive Movement, which feared that becoming involved in the war could threaten the political and social gains it had achieved over the last dozen years. The war was favored by "Big Business," the Progressives warned, and would undermine ***civil liberties***.

The U.S. business community, more closely linked to the British Empire than to Germany, generally supported the Allied cause. In the first two and a half years of the war, New York banks arranged loans of about $2.25 billion to the Allies.

America's neutral stance was additionally complicated by new developments in warfare. The Germans depended on submarines, called U-boats during World War I. Responding to the British blockade of German ports, the German navy banned all ships from a war zone around the British Isles. Any neutral ships in that area could be sunk without warning, the Germans warned.

Wilson claimed that civilians had the right to travel freely to the warring nations on passenger ships without fearing for their lives. The U-boat blockade violated this right, and when the Germans sunk the *Lusitania* on May 7, 1915, killing 123 Americans, Wilson and the American public were outraged. Wilson protested that the Germans must cease their attacks.

Wilson's secretary of state, William Jennings Bryan, was a firm advocate of neutrality. He thought that Wilson's demands on the Germans were unrealistic. The President's position, Bryan feared, would lead the country into war, and Bryan resigned shortly after the sinking of the *Lusitania*.

Despite the American protests, the Germans did not change their policy immediately. On March 24, 1916, the Germans sunk the *Sussex*, killing eighty people, including four Americans. This was enough. Wilson issued his **ultimatum**: Germany would cease its submarine warfare or

Lusitania *headlines*

the United States would break off relations with the country. Germany did agree to stop the attacks, but it reserved the right to resume them if the United States did not persuade the British to lift their blockade.

As the conflict escalated, many Americans believed their country could not remain neutral indefinitely. Former President Teddy Roosevelt, for example, deplored the position taken by Wilson. The conduct of the German Army in neutral Belgium outraged him, and he thought if Americans entered the war, they would have a better chance at shaping the peace terms to end the conflict.

The Progressive Movement

Poster for the movie version of Upton Sinclair's The Jungle

The last twenty-five years of the nineteenth century saw rapid growth in the U.S. economy. Developments in industry fueled much of that growth, as businesses had international markets available for their products. The West was settled, so there were more opportunities for business within the domestic borders as well.

Not everyone shared in the new wealth and opportunities that the growth brought. Women could not vote. The mentally ill were often locked away without treatment, and working conditions were often dangerous. Rather than just sit by and do nothing, many social activists (the progressives) saw the need and decided they could do something about what they saw as society's ills. They felt that individuals and the government working together could make society better for all. The reformers started working on local government levels, but proceeded up the political ladder until they were bringing about change on the national level.

The reformers had help. Muckrakers were writers who tried to stir people to action through their words. One of the most important was Upton Sinclair. His book *The Jungle* brought the despicable conditions of the meat-packing industry to the public's attention.

One of the most important successes of the Progressive Movement was women's suffrage. In 1920, the nineteenth amendment, giving women the right to vote, was passed. Women could now elect the

President and those who would represent them in Congress—the ones responsible for creating the laws that affected their lives.

The late 1800s and early 1900s also saw a large rise in the number of immigrants, and the Progressives saw that they were often the victims of society. They were among the poorest of the population and had no one to whom to turn. Thanks to people such as Jane Addams and her Hull House in Chicago, some were able to get the help they needed.

The Progressive Movement was also successful in getting food and drug laws passed, getting new amendments to the Constitution that brought a new way to elect senators ratified, and starting a conservation movement.

Not all issues were dealt with successfully, however. The courts routinely blocked efforts to reform child labor laws. And the needs of blacks and Native Americans were still largely ignored, perhaps the biggest failure of the movement.

Other Americans agreed with Roosevelt and thought the country needed to make preparations for eventual intervention in the war. In 1915, for example, a group of men connected with the military set up a privately funded camp in upper New York State to train young men as officers.

Wilson also took action to prepare the country for war. In December 1915, he requested $500 million from Congress to add ten battleships and a hundred submarines to the U.S. Navy over the next ten years. The following year, Congress responded to Wilson's request and doubled the size of the army to 200,000 men. It also enlarged the merchant marine fleet.

The President, however, clung to the hope that the United

Child laborers in Indiana Glass Works, Midnight, Indiana, 1908

Wilson declaring war

Navy recruiting poster, 1917

States might remain apart from the war in Europe. In January 1916, Wilson sent a personal representative, Edward M. House, to negotiate with the warring parties in Europe. By this time, the war had cost more than four million lives and the governments of France, Great Britain, and Germany had depleted their financial reserves. On the Eastern Front, Russia's regime was tottering and would be toppled by a revolution the following year.

House returned with a proposal to present to Wilson, although it was essentially a plan developed by the British. It called for the Americans to act as a mediator, presiding over a peace conference. Before the conference would start, however, the warring enemies would have to withdraw their troops to the prewar battle lines. The British knew, however, that the Germans would never agree to these terms. As it turned out, Wilson himself doubted the realism of this proposal, and he modified it into a general statement that the Americans were willing to mediate the conflict.

The war in Europe was the main issue in Wilson's reelection campaign in 1916, which was bitterly contested. The Republican candidate, U.S. Supreme Court Justice Charles Evans Hughes, campaigned on the issue of increasing American preparedness for war. Wilson argued that his policies already had increased American preparedness. With America strong, Wilson said, the chances were improved that its military would not need to be used. Many observers expected that Hughes would win the election, but when the late returns from California and Ohio were counted, Wilson was declared the winner.

The war, of course, continued through the U.S. election, and by

December 1916, the situation was desperate for all the countries involved. Germany was being strangled by the British blockade, and feared political and social collapse if the war continued much longer. At the end of January, Germany declared that it would no longer be bound by its pledge to the United States. It would resume its blockade of Great Britain.

This might not have been enough to force the United States into the war, but an intercepted piece of diplomatic correspondence was. The so-called "Zimmerman telegram" was a proposal from the German undersecretary of foreign affairs to the German ambassador in Mexico City, encouraging Mexico to declare war on the United States.

This appeared to be a clear threat to the United States, and while Mexico would probably not have been persuaded by the Germans, the Zimmerman telegram was the last straw for the Wilson administration. On April 3, 1917, the President went to Congress, pledging to fight for democracy and "for the peace and safety of all nations." He received a standing ovation, and the Congress voted for war with little dissent.

The United States' powers were now thoroughly at work in the rest of the world. From economic influence and indirect political pressure, America had progressed to direct military involvement. America's entrance onto the global stage was complete.

German warship

1619 A Dutch ship trades twenty Africans to the Jamestown colonists. These first Africans are treated as indentured servants.

1850 The Clayton-Bulwer Treaty provides the legal basis for a canal to be built across the Isthmus of Panama by Great Britain and the United States.

1882 General Ulises Heureaux is inaugurated president of the Dominican Republic.

1846–1848 Mexican-American War

Terminals used in the building of the Panama Canal

September 14, 1901 President William McKinley dies after being shot. Vice President Theodore Roosevelt succeeds him.

November 18, 1903 Panamanian special envoy Bunau-Varilla and United States Secretary of State Hay sign treaty establishing legal basis for constructing the Panama Canal.

1902 Great Britain and Germany impose blockade on Venezuela to collect debts.

1898 United States defeats Spain in the Spanish-American War, taking control of former Spanish colonies of Puerto Rico and the Philippines.

1904 Theodore Roosevelt formulates the Roosevelt Corollary.

July 1912 Nicaraguan nationalists attack Managua. United States sends a flotilla of warships with Marines to help crush revolt.

1910 Mexican revolution begins.

June 28, 1914 Serbian student assassinates Austrian Archduke Franz Ferdinand in Sarajevo. Escalating responses to murder among European powers leads to World War I.

1911 Insurgents funded by the United Fruit Company try to topple Honduran President Miguel Davila. Chinese emperor is overthrown the same year.

A 1913 warship

1916 President Woodrow Wilson sends General John Pershing and 11,000 troops to Mexico to look for Pancho Villa.

November 29, 1916 United States announces its occupation of Dominican Republic, creating a military government that lasts until September 1924.

May 7, 1915 German submarine sinks *Lusitania*, killing 123 Americans.

August 1916 United States purchases Virgin Islands from Denmark for $25 million.

April 3, 1917 President Woodrow Wilson declares war on Germany, and the United States enters World War I.

FURTHER READING

Brands, H. W. *TR: The Last Romantic.* New York: Basic Books, 1997.

Morris, Edmund. *Theodore Rex.* New York: Random House, 2001.

Moss, George Donelson. *America in the Twentieth Century.* Upper Saddle River, N.J.: Prentice Hall, 2004.

Munro, Dana G. *Intervention and Dollar Diplomacy in the Caribbean 1900–1921.* Princeton, N.J.: Princeton University Press, 1964.

Rauchway, Eric. *Murdering McKinley.* New York: Hill and Wang, 2003.

Reckner, James R. *Teddy Roosevelt's Great White Fleet.* Annapolis, Md.: Naval Institute Press, 1988.

Richard, Alfred Charles, Jr. *The Panama Canal in American National Consciousness, 1870–1990.* New York: Garland Publishing, 1990.

Zimmerman, Warren. *First Great Triumph: How Five Americans Made Their Country a World Power.* New York: Farrar, Straus and Giroux, 2002.

FOR MORE INFORMATION

Brownpride.com:
www.brownpride.com/history/default.asp

Canal Museum:
www.canalmuseum.com/

Cyber Learning-world:
www.cyberlearning-world.com/lessons/ushistory/lpimperialism1.htm

Harold B. Lee Library:
www.lib.byu.edu/~rdh/wwi/

The National Portrait Gallery:
www.npg.si.edu/exh/roosevelt/

Small Planet:
www.smplanet.com/imperialism/joining.html

Spartacus Educational:
www.spartacus.schoolnet.co.uk/FWW.htm

Time Magazine:
www.time.com/time/time100/leaders/profile/troosevelt.html

The United Nations Educational, Scientific, and Cultural Organization:
www.unesco.org/culture/publications/caribbean/html_eng/index_en.shtml

Vincent Voice Library:
www.lib.msu.edu/vincent/presidents/taft

The White House:
www.whitehouse.gov/history/presidents/tr26.html

Windows on Haiti:
www.windowsonhaiti.com/

INDEX

BIOGRAPHIES

AUTHOR

Eric Schwartz is a journalist living in Binghamton, New York. He received his bachelor's degree in Russian and journalism from Michigan State University and his master's degree in international relations from Syracuse University.

SERIES CONSULTANT

Dr. Jack N. Rakove is a professor of history and American studies at Stanford University, where he is director of American studies. The winner of the 1997 Pulitzer Prize in history, Dr. Rakove is the author of *The Unfinished Election of 2000, Constitutional Culture and Democratic Rule,* and *James Madison and the Creation of the American Republic.* He is also the president of the Society for the History of the Early American Republic.

PICTURE CREDITS